Published by Creative Education
and Creative Paperbacks
P.O. Box 227, Mankato, Minnesota 56002
Creative Education and Creative Paperbacks
are imprints of The Creative Company
www.thecreativecompany.us

Design by The Design Lab
Production by Joe Kahnke
Art direction by Rita Marshall
Printed in the United States of America

Photographs by Alamy (age fotostock, Picture
Partners), Corbis (Christian Ziegler/Minden Pictures,
ZSSD/Minden Pictures), Dreamstime (Bowie15, Foxy-
joshi, Ifocus, Isselee, Vladimir Korostyshevskiy, David
Morton, Mtilghma, Sergey Uryadnikov), Shutterstock
(Shackleford-Photography, Vikulin, wojciech wojcik)

Library of Congress Cataloging-in-Publication Data
Bodden, Valerie.
Iguanas / Valerie Bodden.
p. cm. — (Amazing animals)
Summary: A basic exploration of the appearance, be-
havior, and habitat of iguanas, the North and South
American dewlapped reptiles. Also included is a story
from folklore explaining why iguanas live in trees.
Includes bibliographical references and index.
ISBN 978-1-60818-754-6 (hardcover)
ISBN 978-1-62832-362-7 (pbk)
ISBN 978-1-56660-796-4 (eBook)
1. Iguanas—Juvenile literature.
QL666.L25 2017
597.95—dc23   2016004787

CCSS: RI.1.1, 2, 4, 5, 6, 7; RI.2.2, 5, 6, 7, 10;
RI.3.1, 5, 7, 8; RF.1.1, 3, 4; RF.2.3, 4

HC 9 8 7 6 5 4 3 2
First Edition PBK 9 8 7 6 5 4 3 2 1

AMAZ·NG ANIMALS

IGUANAS

BY VALERIE BODDEN

CREATIVE EDUCATION · CREATIVE PAPERBACKS

Some green iguanas are brown (below), but Fiji banded ones (opposite) are green

Iguanas are big lizards. Like all lizards, they are reptiles. Reptiles are **cold-blooded** animals with scaly bodies. There are about 40 kinds of iguanas in the world.

cold-blooded having bodies that are always as warm or as cold as the air around them

Most iguanas have a flap of skin called a dewlap under their chin. They have a long tail and strong legs. An iguana has a spiky back. Most iguanas are green, brown, or gray. Some can change color. They get darker when they are cold. They turn a lighter color when they are hot.

The dewlap of a healthy iguana is soft and able to move easily

The smallest iguanas are shorter than a ruler. But the longest iguanas are seven feet (2.1 m) from their nose to the tip of their tail! The heaviest iguanas can weigh 30 pounds (13.6 kg).

Galápagos marine iguanas can grow to weigh 20–30 pounds (9.1–13.6 kg)

Iguanas live in North America and South America. They live on some islands, too. Iguanas like places that are hot. Most make their homes in forests. Some live in hot, dry lands called deserts.

Iguanas warm their bodies in the sunshine—until they get too hot

Iguanas eat their soft food whole, without chewing it

Most iguanas eat fruits, flowers, and leaves. Sometimes they eat **insects**. One kind of iguana even dives into the water to munch on seaweed!

insects small animals with three body parts and six legs

A female iguana digs a nest where she lays all her eggs

Mother iguanas lay about 20 to 70 eggs. The baby iguanas all **hatch** at the same time. They live in a group for a little while. As they grow, the iguanas shed their skin. Most iguanas live 15 to 20 years in the wild.

hatch come out of an egg

An iguana's clawed feet help it climb slippery branches

Many iguanas spend their time in trees. They can fall 40 feet (12.2 m) without getting hurt! Iguanas like trees with branches that hang over water. They can get away from a **predator** by dropping into the water. They use their strong tails to swim away.

predator an animal that kills and eats other animals

Sometimes iguanas gather in big groups. They lie together in the sun. But male iguanas may fight each other over female iguanas.

Marine (sea) iguanas usually make up the largest groups

Some people keep iguanas as pets. But they can be hard to care for. Other people visit iguanas at zoos or in the wild. It is fun to watch these long-tailed, tree-dwelling lizards!

With good food and care, a pet iguana can live several years

An Iguana Story

Why do iguanas live in trees? People in North America told a story about this. They said one day, Iguana heard a cry for help. But he didn't ask what was wrong. So a god hit him and threw him in the river. Iguana climbed out of the river and hid in a tree. He has lived there ever since.

god a being thought to have special powers and control over the world

Read More

Bowman, Chris. *Iguanas*. Minneapolis: Bellwether Media, 2015.

Raum, Elizabeth. *Green Iguanas*. Mankato, Minn.: Amicus, 2015.

Websites

Enchanted Learning: Iguanas
http://www.enchantedlearning.com/subjects/reptiles
/lizard/Iguanaprintout.shtml
This site has iguana facts and a picture to print out and color.

San Diego Zoo Kids: Fiji Banded Iguana
http://kids.sandiegozoo.org/animals/reptiles/fiji-banded-iguana
Learn more about the Fiji banded iguana.

Note: Every effort has been made to ensure that the websites listed above are suitable for children, that they have educational value, and that they contain no inappropriate material. However, because of the nature of the Internet, it is impossible to guarantee that these sites will remain active indefinitely or that their contents will not be altered.

Index